T0370414

WINE
&
WORD PLAY

A POETRY BOOK & WRITING JOURNAL

BY LOC'D

authorHOUSE·

AuthorHouse™
1663 Liberty Drive
Bloomington, IN 47403
www.authorhouse.com
Phone: 833-262-8899

Published by AuthorHouse 08/19/2024

ISBN: 979-8-8230-2939-1 (sc)
ISBN: 979-8-8230-2938-4 (e)

Contents

Contents

Foreword/Dedication

This book is not mine…it's ours. We wrote it collaboratively. Collected these words month after month of enjoying wine and a good time at Durham's first black female owned urban winery, **Melanated Wine** during the monthly *"Poetry Night Experience"*. I'm so glad this book provides the opportunity to look back over the wonderfully creative and collaborative poems that were penned since 2022. Writing each one of these poems (with the help of your words) was such an experience and it was all the more special because you were there. A special expression of gratitude to LaShonda & Seneca Modest for opening their arms and their beautiful space for us to uncork culture, creativity, and community. As you read each poem, I hope it makes you smile and reminisce as much as it makes me. I'm Loc'd but please never forget…you all are the keys. Stay loc'd in with me and as always…show love.

Loc'd

How to engage with this book

Throughout this book, you will notice a pattern in its format. There will be: 2 definitions, 2 poems, a picture of sticky notes, and a writing prompt with lined space on which to write. The definitions provided are the titles of the 2 poems that follow. The words were chosen as titles for the poems as they were either particularly unique to my everyday vernacular or they were meaningfully representative of the context of the poem. The poems apart of this book serve as both reading enjoyment and writing examples. Following the poems will be a picture of the sticky notes of the very words given to me at the open mic event that accompanied the poems written. The pictures of these words are being provided not only as a nice graphic, but also as a place to start your writing journey. They serve as an invitation for you to take part in the exercise that I have been doing over the years of using other's words to articulate one's own thoughts. Feel free to incorporate as many or as few of the words as you feel led to in response to each writing prompt. Sometimes we can be at a loss for words. In this book, there are many to be found. I hope you find strength in your pen and wonder in this artistic journey along with me.

1. **_Demiurgic_** (adjective, derivative of demiurge)

   – Being of a powerful creative force or personality.

2. **_Befreeing_** (verb, derivative of befree)

   – To make or set free; liberate; deliver; release.

Demiurgic

*In a **nostalgic** moment*
*I **quiver** at the **vision** of my former self*
The fragrance of carnations
***Captivating** to my senses **elevate** me to another plane*
***Uncork** memories I thought I'd forgotten*
*A time when happiness and **love** eluded me*
Embarrassed at how I indulged in sipping
on a devolved version of self
*Diluted destiny dripping like **bordeaux** off drunken tongues*
*Disconnected from how **extraordinary** I was to become*
*Lisping and lacking **energy** to devote patience*
*to successful **transformation***
But I am grateful for elevation
*Ability to be **malleable** and **demiurgic***
No longer simply a character but the creator in my story
*Fluidly molding an **expansive** new universe around me*
*It's astounding how **sensational** belief in self*
*Can be an **achievement** that seems unattainable*
*But in becoming **empowered***
I eject imposter
Enjoy the fruits of my labor
***Orange, strawberry** sweetly savored*
*Blooming in **connection** with favor*
Feeling blessed to exist in present
And accept myself as my greatest gift

Befreeing

❧

Love is *lovely*
When love *befreeing*
Liberating me from *egregious* error
Of ignoring how *powerful* I am
Helping me *understand* that love can be *gentle*
Less clenched fist and more open caress
That can soothingly *finesse* all my rough edges
The sands of time eroded away by *grief*
Healing me piece by piece
Until *peace* reenters my spirit as *advent* season
Birthing gift of *grateful* heart
Unwrapping *happiness* like Christmas morning
Dawning *limitless* possibilities for me to find my footing
Grounding me in the reality that I am deserving
Of soaring to new heights with a *first class* love
I'm *done* with coach playing games with my heart
I'm tackling my trust issues and building *stability*
Recognizing that *timing* and *integrity* are everything
How receiving a kiss and one *pinky* promise
Give sentiments of "I *gotcha*" more
valuable than five golden rings
No longer captive to the ghost of crippling past
I release my demons and *manifest*
A *love* that will be a gift that keeps on giving
A *Christmas* miracle in July
Faithful, fruitful, and freeing for all lifetime

Uncork

Expansive

Captivating

demiurgic

Successful

Vision

BLESSED

Devote.

Malleable

nostalgic

Transformation

Elevate

CHAIR

Prompt One: Write the creation story of an evolved version of yourself OR write the liberation story from a past version of yourself (or both ☺)

_____

_____

_____

_____

_____

_____

_____

_____

_____

_____

_____

_____

3. **_Euphemism_** (noun)

 – a mild or more pleasant expression used as substitution for a harsh or offensive statement.

4. **_Paradigm_** (noun)

 – A set of values, basic assumptions or systems of thought that are commonly accepted by a specified community.

Euphemism

Woman
An **energy** which **transcends**
The expression of **joy** and **blessings**
Exemplifying **peace** surpassing understanding
Empowered with **endurance** that's unmatched
An **unbothered** breathing **euphemism** for "unfuckwitable"
Unforgettable **muse**
A **loss** if mishandled
Because nothing holds a candle to her shine
Women be **divine**
Life drips from her lips
Agape exhaled through her nose
And **juxtaposed** she takes your breath away
Perfect balance of sweet and **sultry**
Sommelier in her own right
Finding the perfect blend for her life
Of **motivation, faith** and **thankfulness**
She be nothing less than greatness
Breaking molds, glass ceilings, even sound barriers
A larger than life **onomatopoeia**
A sound that speaks louder than words
She be woman
And she be a wonder

Paradigm

Her essence is ***aromatic***
You sense her before you see her
*Captivating **ebony** cosmo*
*Sweet and **seductive***
Rooted** in **love
*Blooming **dreams***
*Her **laughter** be **raindrops** watering landscapes*
*Creating **paradise** in every place she graces*
*Her **unique sweetness** softens hardened tongues*
Switching any speech that seeks to undermine her
To songs of praise
*Her strength shifts **paradigm***
She breaks ground and ceilings
*While **grounding** and healing*
*She **balance baggage** and **boundaries***
Packing thunder in her thighs
*Giving **longevity** to her stride*
*Making room for her to **manifest** vision*
*With air of **tranquility** she suffocates stress*
*Lays it to rest in **urn***
For she's earned this peace
She burns with passion
Rises from ashes
Phoenix flying
***Balloon** gliding*
On winds of change

Prompt Two: Write about a euphemism you feel needs a paradigm shift

_____

_____

_____

_____

_____

_____

_____

_____

_____

_____

_____

_____

5. **Steatopygic** (noun)

   – state of having substantial levels of tissue on the buttocks and thighs, especially in women.

6. **Dilapidated** (adjective)

   – fallen into a state of partial ruin due to age or neglect; elegantly deteriorated.

Steatopygic

*Humble beginnings as delicate **flower***
Incredible soul
***Radiance live** in her*
Aura** blooms as she **manifests joy, love & faith
***Together** a **palette** of vibrant living color*
*An **essence** of **strength***
*She walks in **happiness***
***Hypocrite** hate her **passion** for life*
*And the **value** she add to the world*
*How she stand **distinguished** against strife*
Steadfast, unwavering, never becoming unfurled
Called home** to **ones
*That mold her **steatopygic** stature*
***Awesome** is her birthright*
***Blessed** through her right to birth others*
She is love
She is light
She is mother

Dilapidated

***Divine** feminine*
***Beautiful** unspoken*
*Reserved **wine***
***Dragonfly** who lends her wings*
So seeds may fly
Mother you are…
***Hustler**, healer, her*
***Sensual**, sage, savior*
*Even when **dilapidated**, devastated and destroyed*
You rebuild again and again
Stronger and safer than before
*You **learn** and lean on the lesson*
*Lending **love** as a blessing*
*An example of examination and **exploration***
Evidence of welcome and warmth and wonder
A woman, goddess, guide
Mother you are

AURA

Radiance

Value

incredible

Passion

Hypocrite

essence

Called

manifest

distinguished

Strength

Steatopygic

live

HOME

Happiness

Prompt Three: Write a letter to a mother in your life. This can be a thank you letter, a confession, a dream, expressing a need, an ode, whatever your heart needs to express (*i.e. your mother, mother earth, yourself as a mother, any mother figure*)

_____

_____

_____

_____

_____

_____

_____

_____

_____

_____

_____

_____

7. ***Equanimity*** (noun)

   – mental calmness, composure and evenness
   of temper especially in difficult situations

8. ***Serendipity*** (noun)

   – an unplanned fortunate discovery

Equanimity

I decided this will be my first year of **firsts**
My **evolution** depends on my **intentional** attempt at **courage**
To find **pleasure** in **consistency**
Develop **phenomenal passion** for exploring
the parts of myself I considered
cretinous
All along simply misunderstood
Lacking the **analytical lust** to learn more about my layers
I lost ability to adore my lovely imperfections
But this new direction of self-love
Is **joyful**
Serendipitous
Reminiscent of a past life where I existed as **majestic princess**
Leading with **love** as my rule
A jewel in the rough more **bling** than **dust**
Radiating **radiance** that resonates like sun
Healing **vibration** to nurture my animal
instinct like **veterinarian**
I'm thankful for **equanimity** in embracing
all I was and all I am to be
So the first firsts I will pursue
is the **vibe** that causes this **rose** to bloom bigger...better...braver
Present behavior dictated by **decorum** daringly dedicated
To putting myself first
For the first time

Serendipity

After years of daydreams
*I awoke to a scene of serene **serendipity***
Happenstance found me
*A mere **human** in alien **territory***
Empowering me with ability to
***Expeditiously** embark on journey of self discovery*
*I **wonder** where the **fork** in the road will lead me*
*Down **toxic** trail tainted with **maleficent** energy*
*Seeking to drain my **power***
*Depleting my **dopamine***
*Deny me access to knowing I am **needed***
Rendering me depressed and devoid of joy
Or...
*Will it put me on **perfect** path for **manifesting** my **passion***
*Remind me to be hopeless **romantic** for life more fulfilling*
*Permit me **vulnerability** to fall in **love***
*with all the **women** within me*
*The woman of **faith** following a **humble** path of purpose*
*The hard working woman exemplifying **excellence***
*The dedicated woman defined by devotion and **consistency***
*The **unbothered** woman with **uncorked** and unmatched energy*
*The **decadent** woman indulging in fine*
***chocolate** and expensive wine*
*The fun loving woman who can **socialize,** dance **Zumba** and*
*enjoy Parliament **Funkadelic** in the summertime*
Eclectic and energetic
Moving and magnetic
More than mere human
A spirit in human form
And alien to the norm

Needed

Vulnerability

FORK

Humble

dopamine

expeditiously

Decadent

TOXIC

SERENDIPITY

Human

territory

MALEFICENT

Perfect

Romantic

Prompt Four: Write about a journey you want to make to an unknown place (earthly, celestial, or in the depths of the universe). Be descriptive. What do you think you'll see? What challenges may you face? How do you plan to show up for yourself on this journey?

_____

_____

_____

_____

_____

_____

_____

_____

_____

_____

_____

_____

9. ***Voluptuous*** (adjective)

    – given to or spent in enjoyment of luxury, pleasure, or sensual gratification.

10. ***Rapturous*** (adjective)

    – A state or experience of being carried away by overwhelming emotion

Voluptuous

__God__ looked down on all my limbs and __ligaments__
Scattered and sacred
__brown, lovely and complicated__
And spoke __softly__ over my mold
"This one will be bold!
Filled with __passion__ for __freedom__ because the world will be cold
The __black__ night may try to imprison her light
But I'll equip her with __perseverance__ to prevail in her fight
Fortify her with strong-will and __self-love__
But she won't be __withdrawn__
__Pain__ won't sour her __sweet__ spirit
For __sugar__ run through her veins
Her arms will remain open to __cuddle__ all life's blessings
And she'll grow greater __integrity__ through all life's lessons
__Happenstance__ encounters won't lessen her __element__ of __trust__
or __voluptuous__ lust to embrace life in all
its __fantastic__ fullness and flaws
The __amazing__ faith planted within her
will sprout up like wild flowers
And __boy!__
The __prosperity__ that pours from her heart will overflow!

Rapturous

I am **blessed**
Divine blessed me to be **unique** and **eccentric**
But different ain't always seen as **valuable**
Too many **persuaded** that **luxury** is only
attached to earthly tangibles
Can't **contemplate** the richness of my **grace**
Too **complacent** to compound interest
enough to invest in my good stock
Too callus to **welcome** the decadence of my **chocolate** in
Gloss over the **salvation** given through my **velvet** kisses
Lacking vision to **dream** of the **tranquility**
that abides in my arms
Elevate your mind
Become **conscientious** of the signs
Let north star bring you **faith** and **Taurus** moon be your guide
Decide to walk **starboard** side
Find the right to free yourself of **pipe**
dreams that left you behind
Awaken a new perspective with **rapturous** reception
A direction that fosters **friendship** and cultivates connection
A genuinely magical space that grants feelings so
Supercalifragilisticexpialidocious
You'll wonder why you never chose this path before
So my prayer be
That you embrace it
Embrace me
Let love do the rest
Then we can both be blessed
Ase'

Ligaments

Voluptuous

complicated

Prosperity

ELEMENT

Sugar

HAPPENSTANCE

Cuddle

Trust

Withdrawn

Pain

Perseverance

Freedom

Complicated

Prompt Five: Write a love letter to yourself in third person thanking yourself for being who you are!

_____

_____

_____

_____

_____

_____

_____

_____

_____

_____

_____

_____

_____

11. **_Resilient_** (adjective)

  – the ability to withstand and respond to challenges not just in a way that helps you survive but also recover quickly

12. **_Tranquil_** (adjective)

  – free from disturbance of the mind or spirit; peaceful without violence or worry

Resilient

*I'm **fed up!***
*Fed up with being **resilient** for causes that don't consider me*
*Tired of having **perseverance** for nightmare dressed as **dream***
*Taunted by **temptation** to **wonder** what could be*
*Waning my **strength** to see what is*
*A **legacy** no longer **holy** or **wholesome***
*A **heritage** of hurt*
*Banking on bankrupting my **prosperity***
*Leaving me less **faith**, less **joy**, less **forgiveness***
***Denial** blinding me from the obvious*
That I'd given much more than deserved
*When did I become **satisfied** with this **sacrifice** of self?*
*How do I **balance** the **growth** I seek and the **grief** I've found?*
*Being bound won't help me become **blessed***
The sacrifice must shift from self to
*everything less than **excellence***
Because excellence is who I am
And I deserve more of me

Tranquil

*I am on a **voyage** to my soft era*
***Plush feminine** space*
where I'm not singularly defined by strength
*But graced with **acceptance** of the **whole** of me*
*My **tranquil spirit***
*My **sexy mind***
*My **fantastic** body*
*A place where I freely **breathe love***
*And exhale **disappointment***
***Clean** house of anything less than decadent reassurance*
Settle self-love sweetly on my taste buds like
strawberry** covered in **chocolate
Treat myself like the treat I am
Knowing my flaws don't make me less than
*Where my good, bad, beautiful and ugly abide in **harmony***
A melody that manifests my higher self
My happier self
My healed self
Soft, secure and serene

Voyage

Love, Disappointment

PLush

Strawberry

tranquil

clean

spirit

Fantastic

Acceptance

Whole

sexy

Breathe.

Harmony

Prompt Six: Write about a sacrifice (*personally or universally*) that has been made that you simply cannot accept

_____

_____

_____

_____

_____

_____

_____

_____

_____

_____

_____

_____

13. **Intrepid** (adjective)

    – resolute fearlessness, adventurous fortitude and endurance

14. **Insurmountable** (noun)

    – Too great to be dealt with successfully; incapable of being overcome

Intrepid

What is **love**?
Love be **strength**
Empowering **intrepid journeys**
Where skies & **stardust** are no longer the limit
Eyes wide shut clearly see constellation
found when **friend** becomes **beloved**
Delicate **slide** between companion and **passion**
Building **brick** foundation preventing falling stars
What is **love**?
Love be elevated **taste**
Filet mignon and red wine
Rich, hearty, select
Unleash virgin palettes to high **society**
Embrace a higher me
Claim seats at tables I was too reserved
to reserve my rightful seat at
Exchange meager means for **empress** new clothes
Gorgeous, royal, righteous
Illuminate the **celebration** I am
What is **love**?

Love be fierce
Dangerous **dragon** in protection of peace
Filled with fire, never **folding, chair** of
alliance to unfold the **truth**
Fierce and frisky
Hips twisting freely like **soca** rhythms and freedom ringing
Inhibitions leaving wherever love be lingering
Fierce and flippant
Switching **oops** to optimism
Making hap hazard **hopeful**
Lubricate life lines and soul ties
unlocking forgiveness that gives greater
…**love**

Insurmountable

It's morning....
And the sun melts my dreams away
*I **shift** between sleep and tight rope walker*
Saunter through life overcome with an
insurmountable perplexed mood
I ponder
***Striving** to see the **silver** lining*
*When **sonder reflection** erases **borders** in my mind*
*I travel beyond the **edges** of time*
*Find **friends** I never knew*
*From the birth of **Brooklyn** hip-hop*
*To the birth of nations in **Ethiopia***
*A utopia where **vivacious melanated radiance** shines*
Love** is the **vibe
***Integrity** is integral part of our design*
Growth** like **buckeye
Bearing fruit in fall as we rise
Breaths rise and fall
*Carry me back to **sweet** slumber*
*I become **ostrich** with head on sandman's lap*
Chest fall and rise
***Passionate** dreams arise as I fall deeper*
*Feeling more and more **vulnerable***
Aroused by dreams of love, lust and unity

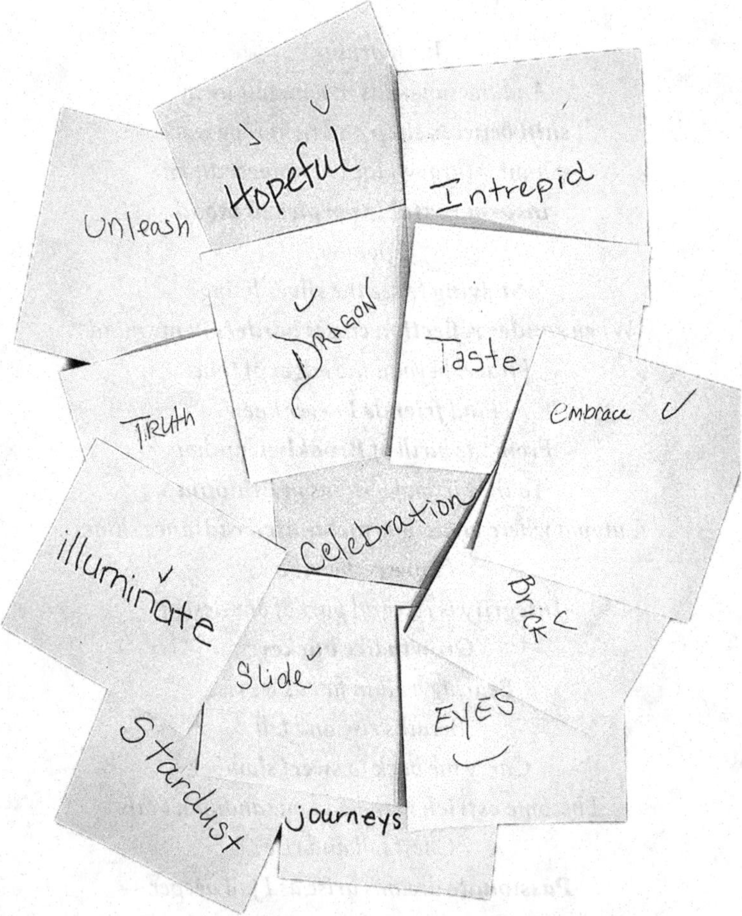
Hopeful
Unleash
Intrepid
DRAGON
Taste
TRUTH
Embrace
Celebration
illuminate
Brick
Slide
EYES
Stardust
journeys

Prompt Seven: Write about a fear you formerly felt was insurmountable that you are now ready and intrepid enough to overcome

_____

_____

_____

_____

_____

_____

_____

_____

_____

_____

_____

_____

_____

_____

15. **_Audacity_** (noun)

   - a willingness to disregard restraint to take bold risks that will likely shock people

16. **_Genesis_** (noun)

   - the origin or creative beginning of something seemingly small but never unimportant

Audacity

❦

3....2....1....
Cheers to new beginnings
Like **cherry** blossoms and new wine
Budding and bubbling with expectation
Blessed and brimming over with **forgiveness**
Allowing **harmony** and **love** to bloom
Rooted in **alignment**
Releasing **pressure** to condense or conform
Comforted by a refreshing point of view
A **vibe** never felt before
Beautiful and renewing
Through this **evolution**
Audacity to dream again is harvested
Bigger and more vibrant than before
There is so much in store
For self, **love, family** and friends
This new vision doesn't end
But seems to go on forever
And I am forever grateful for greater **intimacy**
Entangled in moments of discovery
Unfolding **exotic** experiences
Exposing me to greater possibilities
Quickening my steps towards exploration and glee
More than a **musical**
But a theme song for a new era
New year
New me

Genesis

*I was **brokenhearted***
***Tired,** heavy, torn*
Depleted and worn
*No longer **fulfilled***
Emptied of my former vibrance
*Losing the longing to be **optimistic***
But I miss the melodies of my former self
***Music** mighty and soul stirring*
Now I'm ready to return
Put my scattered pieces back together like Pangea
Become whole again
Become home again
*A **prolific** revival*
Begin again
*Call me **Genesis***
I am triumphant new beginnings
*Drape me in **purple***
I am royal, blessed, favored
Rising from ashes
*Bringing all the **smoke***
***Sensual,** spiritual, healed*
Back like I never left
But more than I was before
Broken never felt better
And peace never felt more whole

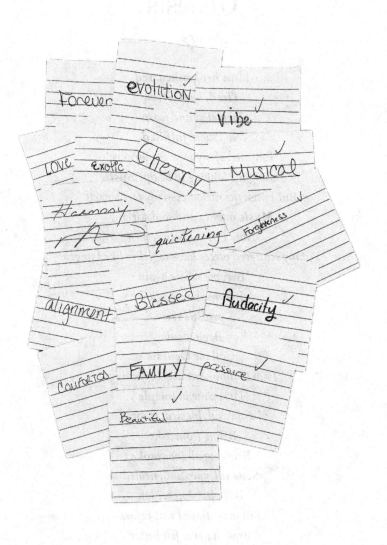

Prompt Eight: Write a list poem about things you have on your bucket list or about opportunities you wished you would have taken but missed

_____

_____

_____

_____

_____

_____

_____

_____

_____

_____

_____

_____

_____

_____

_____

17. ***Flower Bomb*** (noun)

– a cluster of wildflower seeds placed in clay pods and planted in urban areas to create an explosive revival of flora life

18. ***Pulchritudinous*** (adjective)

– breathtakingly beautiful delighting the senses

Flower Bomb

I can tell you've grown **tired** of the **nonchalant** stance of society
This life is but a **simulation**
Take the right pill to **uncork new revelation**
Time is over to play small
Your greatness isn't a **game**
Unlock new territories
Discover a new name
Identify as **love**
Let it overflow from your palms
Plant **flower bombs**
Find **freedom** as native wildflower
Occupy all the spaces they said you weren't suited for
Ground in **gratitude**
Rediscover your **lust** for life
Become embodiment of **delight, full** of vibrance
Excited to spread this joy to the world

Pulchritudinous

*You know what is **beautiful**?*
*My **broken***
*For too long in my **life** the truth eluded me*
I dwelled in deception that I could only be
phenomenal** and **pulchritudinous
If I were perfect
*Robbed of the **grace** to evolve*
*Not permitted to uncover **love** in the lessons*
*Or bask in the blessings that **bubble** up from my blunders*
Nor wonder what wrong my wrong turn saved me from
Now I've come to recognize I'm the sum of all my parts
*Weak and **powerful***
***Inspired** and jaded*
*Restless and resting in **peace** that the pieces of me*
Materialize** more **persistence** and **integrity
*The **freedom** I feel when I get to be myself completely*
Is a feeling like no other
*Like **chocolate** kisses melting gently on my*
lips as I speak sweetly to myself
Unfolding my power
***Flower** into brave blossom*
*Water myself in such an **intentional** way*
*that rain become **irresistible***

Realizing that rain be the only way my
*roots of **resilience** can grow*
Now I glow in a way that blind eyes can see
*Made vow to self to be my own **wifey** for a*
lifelong journey of self-discovery
Learn from my losses
*Admire the **analyst** within*
Which lends me new perspective and insight
*Which is...I am the **GOAT** in my own right*

Aggressive ✓

PEACE

Empower ✓

Embrass

Happiness

Sippin

strong ✓

bordeaux
Carnation

✳ ✳ ✳
✳ Blessed ✳
✳ ✳ ✳

Energy
Connection

Tenderness ✓

restoration ✓   Quinch ✓

Blossom ✓

Anticipation ✓

SKIN ✓

SLOW ✓

Connect
Strawberry
boots
Exit

Prompt Nine: Write about a part of yourself you should celebrate more (i.e. body, heart, character, prevailing over triumph, a flaw that could be an asset)

_____

_____

_____

_____

_____

_____

_____

_____

_____

_____

_____

_____

19. **_Accismus_** (noun)

    – a form of irony where one shows no interest in something while secretly desiring it

20. **_Ambivalent_** (adjective)

    – having opposing feelings regarding something or someone at the same time resulting in being uncertain about how you feel

Accismus

I articulate **contemplation** of escape
In a **vindictive** act my disloyal heart betrays me
Reveals my attempts at retreat to be **accismus**
As the **vehemence** of my desire radiates beyond my self-control
I lose all control absent of you
For you be **purkinje**, the very fiber of my heart
You are my lifeline
Your hold on me will never loosen
And I would not have **chosen** it to
My heart sings **devotion** to only you
The **harmony** hypnotizes me
Melanated melodies dark, rich and deep
Encompassing and **contagious**
To which a cure, I do not seek
On feverish **high** I follow you blindly
Become world **traveler**
Adventuresome and uninhibited
Treading whatever path wherever your love leads
Extending myself with **unconditional** abandon
Feeling **blessed** to freely express this **sweet** surrender
It be like **candy** on my lips
So I dare not taint my tongue with untruths
Not even **low** faint whispers to depart
For **heartbroken** will become my name
Therefore I am **pretty** resolute
Honesty be my only **hope**
To save me from that fate

Ambivalent

For much of my life I felt like an island
Ambivalent waves washing over my shore
Oscillating between the **freedom** and **peace** isolation brings
And the **abundance** of loneliness that surrounded me
The sands of **time** seemingly endless in
this tug of **war** for my allegiance
Deciphering if it be gift or curse to cruise away
from the calm of destitute palms
When the palms of others bruised my **heart**
Left **imprint** that my **worth** was only
weighed by its **loyalty** to others
Those who deemed me more vacation and less **dream** home
Careless corsairs lost on seas of **lust**
Drowning me in **hope** that my **love** was enough for both of us
Convinced me if I called myself martyr
Then we'd resurrect as **unity**
But this mutiny to my self-worth became bitter on my tongue

The mirage of your **magic** melting from my mind
Gave way for **empowerment** to emerge
I am **grateful** we were never **successful**
For there is no **prosperity** in pain
No grace to be gained from turning over
the treasure of my esteem
To undeserving hands
Now I'm recovering all that was stolen by letting go
Finding **perseverance** through releasing
and **zen** in reconnection
Layering self-love like **lotion** rejuvenating all my dry places
Making my soul glow
So retreat to state of island recluse sounds
like perfect place for renewal
Of the vow to my first love....Myself
And reuniting feels so good

DRAGONFLY

Learn

Sensual

exploration

dilapidated

wine

beautiful

divine

Love

Bonding

Hustler

dignity   understanding

Prompt Ten: Write about something you once felt sure about that now brings uncertainty *or* something you were unsure about but now are certain

_____

_____

_____

_____

_____

_____

_____

_____

_____

_____

_____

_____

_____

_____